Was There Really a Gunfight at the O.K. Corral?

And Other Questions about the Wild West

ANN KERNS

ILLUSTRATIONS BY **COLIN W. THOMPSON**

LERNER PUBLICATIONS COMPANY

Minneapolis

Contents

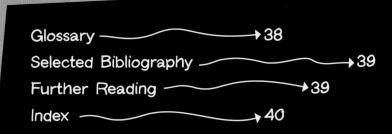

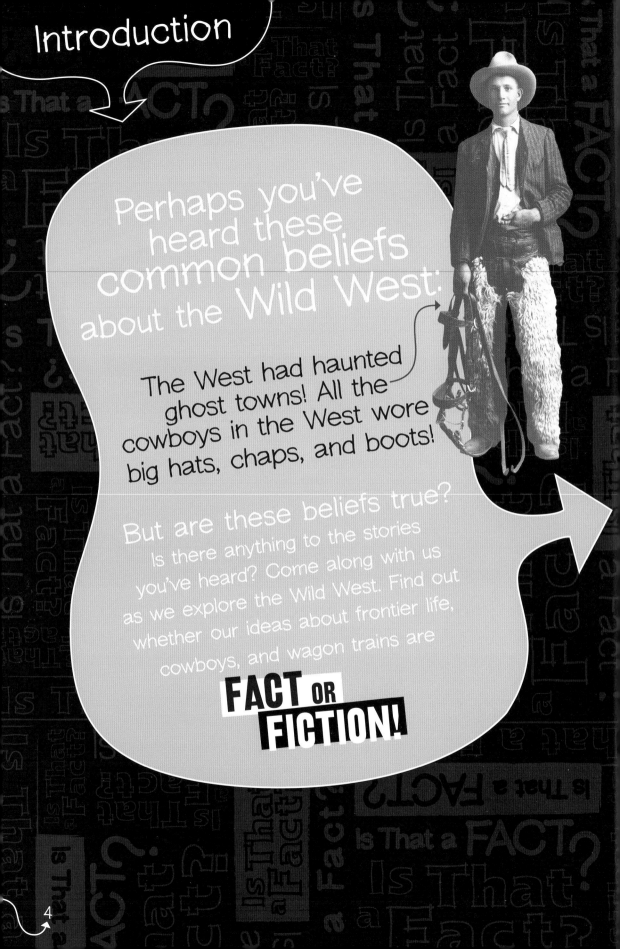

Perhaps you've heard these common beliefs about the Wild West:

The West had haunted ghost towns! All the cowboys in the West wore big hats, chaps, and boots!

But are these beliefs true? Is there anything to the stories you've heard? Come along with us as we explore the Wild West. Find out whether our ideas about frontier life, cowboys, and wagon trains are

FACT OR FICTION!

Did Villains in the Wild West Really Tie Their Victims to Railroad Tracks?

PROBABLY NOT. Some old movies and cartoons show an evil villain dragging a young woman along a deserted stretch of railroad tracks. He ties the woman to the tracks. Then he laughs, twirls his mustache, and runs off. She cries for help as the train speeds toward her. Just in the nick of time, a hero in a white cowboy hat shows up and frees her. Whew! That was close! But chances are it never really happened.

Real-life accounts of victims being tied to railroad tracks are pretty hard to come by. So why are they so common in the movies? Well, people like the thrill of such tales.

The helpless women in these stories are called damsels in distress. Damsels are almost always saved by handsome young men. The villain-damsel-hero scene was used over and over in the 1800s in books and plays. The scenes were so popular that they made the jump to movies in the early 1900s. Soon after that, they began appearing in cartoons.

Bad guys tie a woman to the railroad tracks in *An Oily Scoundrel*, a 1916 film.

Actors reenact the O.K. Corral gunfight for tourists in Tombstone every day!

Was There Really a Gunfight at the O.K. Corral?

YOU BET YOUR BOOTS THERE WAS. It happened on October 26, 1881, in Tombstone, Arizona. But the shootout didn't take place right at the corral (a fenced-in lot for keeping horses). Most of the fighting happened in a passageway between nearby buildings. Storytellers who passed along accounts of the fight must've just thought "gunfight at the O.K. Corral" sounded better than "gunfight in an alley"!

Tombstone was a wild place in those days. The town began in the 1870s as a mining camp. In a few years, its population jumped from about one hundred to fifteen thousand. Peaceful citizens shared the streets with bandits and horse thieves. Many people carried guns. Tombstone was in bad need of some law and order.

In 1881 Virgil Earp became town marshal, or police official. His brothers Wyatt and Morgan and friend Doc Holliday helped him. The Earps and Holliday had a simmering feud with some local outlaws called the Clanton gang.

The Clantons were no-good cattle rustlers. But the Earps and Holliday were no angels either. On the night of October 25, 1881, the two

groups got into several arguments in Tombstone's saloons and gambling halls. Tempers were running hot.

The next day, the Earps and Holliday found some of the Clanton gang on Fremont Street. Words were exchanged, and shots rang out. The gunfight lasted only thirty seconds, but it killed three of the Clantons. Holliday and Morgan and Virgil Earp were wounded.

The gunfight divided Tombstone. Some residents felt that the Earps had done right. Others thought the Earps had overstepped their bounds as lawmen. Wyatt Earp and Doc Holliday were arrested for murder, but the case never went all the way to trial. A judge ruled that the Clantons had brought the gunfight on themselves.

Tombstone's Epitaph

The *Tombstone Epitaph* is a magazine about life in the Wild West. An epitaph is a saying written on a gravestone (or tombstone), such as "Here Lies John Smith." The *Epitaph* has been in business since 1880. Back then, it was a newspaper. In its first issue, publisher John Philip Clum predicted that Tombstone would grow to be a great city. It would, Clum said, come to rival the glories of ancient Rome.

Did Thousands of People Rush to California When Gold Was Discovered There?

YES SIREE, PARDNER. Gold was discovered at Sutter's Mill near the Sierra Nevada (a mountain range) in January 1848. The news didn't make much of a splash until that December, when U.S. president James Polk mentioned it in a speech. By the summer of 1849, the gold rush was on. Treasure hunters, known as forty-niners, flooded into California.

Before 1849, most Californians were Latinos or Native Americans. The gold rush brought about three hundred thousand white Americans, African Americans, Asians, South Americans, Australians, and Europeans to the region. The forty-niners imagined that California literally glittered with gold. They thought they'd be rich in no time.

Many prospectors (people who search for precious metals) panned for gold. Panning is a way to collect loose surface gold. Using metal pans, prospectors scooped up water and dirt from a stream known or thought to contain gold. They swirled the pans until the dirt and water splashed out, leaving the gold behind. Panning was easy and cheap. Prospectors who arrived early in the gold rush made thousands of dollars panning. But in time, competition for panning space grew fierce.

Prospectors began digging gold mines. They tunneled down through hard rock to search for gold. This was hard and dangerous work. Soon large companies took over mining operations. Miners worked for the companies for daily wages. They couldn't keep the gold they found.

But looking for gold wasn't the only way to make money in the gold rush. Many merchants and saloon owners grew rich selling food, clothes, equipment, and entertainment to miners. That trade and commerce helped grow towns and cities in California.

Did You Know?

Gold wasn't the only valuable metal discovered in the West. In 1859, miners discovered silver in the mountains near Virginia City, Nevada (then part of the Utah territory). The huge underground silver deposit became known as the Comstock Lode. Gold was found in the area too.

Did Most Pioneers Live on Farms Miles Away from Their Neighbors?

YES, LOTS OF THEM DID. Most people moved west so they could own a plot of land. They built small houses surrounded by acres of land for crops and livestock. The land was the settlers' only source of money. So they worked hard to make their farms successful.

Hellooo out there!

. . . .

Pioneer families worked all day long, six days a week. Fathers and older children tended the crops and livestock. They mended fences and fixed tools and equipment. Mothers and younger kids cooked, cleaned, sewed, washed clothes by hand, and gardened. All that work kept the family pretty tied to the land. It could get lonely. But when people did find a reason to get together with neighbors, they sure knew how to make the most of it.

Quilting bees were common. At those parties, women got together to sew quilted bedspreads. While they sewed, they chatted and caught up on neighbors' news. Entire communities turned out for barn raisings, where everyone pitched in to help a neighbor put up a new barn or other farm building.

Dances, church socials, and picnics were also popular. Often the highlight of a community's social calendar was a Fourth of July celebration or a county agricultural fair. All these events gave pioneers a chance to have fun, visit with friends, make new friends, and—for young people—meet a future husband or wife.

Sod Sweet Sod

On the prairie, trees only grew near rivers and streams. The rest of the land was one vast stretch of tall, thick grass. The lack of trees meant that lumber was scarce. As a result, many pioneers built their prairie homes out of sod (dirt held together by grass roots). The sod was cut into squares and used like bricks. Sod houses could be very cozy— except when snakes made their way through the grass roofs and dropped onto beds and dinner tables!

Once enough pioneers had settled in an area, they put their money together to build buildings everyone could use. They built churches, stores, and schools. These buildings usually weren't big or fancy, but they were very important to the community. They made settlers feel as if they were planning for the future.

While the schoolhouse was being built, community leaders looked for a teacher to hire. At first, many teachers were men from the East Coast. But then pioneers began hiring local women. Some of these women teachers were very young—not much older than the students themselves. Laura Ingalls Wilder, author of the Little House on the Prairie series, began teaching in South Dakota when she was fifteen.

Laura Ingalls Wilder

Teachers in one-room schoolhouses didn't have a lot to work with. Sometimes they had only one or two books. Some schoolrooms didn't have chalkboards or maps. Students had to bring their own supplies. And during spring planting and fall harvest, the schools were usually empty. But students weren't at home enjoying time off. Most were hard at work in the farm fields!

Not Just in the West

One-room schoolhouses weren't a new idea on the American frontier. They were first built in colonial America in the 1600s. They were also built in Britain, Australia, and Canada. One-room schoolhouses continue to serve some rural or isolated areas.

Were Horses the Most Common Animal Used in the Settlement of the West?

SURPRISINGLY, THE ANSWER IS NO. Cowboys, Native American hunters and warriors, and some U.S. soldiers rode horses. And oxen were used to pull wagons and farm equipment. But much of the West was settled with the help of the lowly mule. In fact, mapmakers, fur trappers, explorers, the military, and settlers all relied on mules.

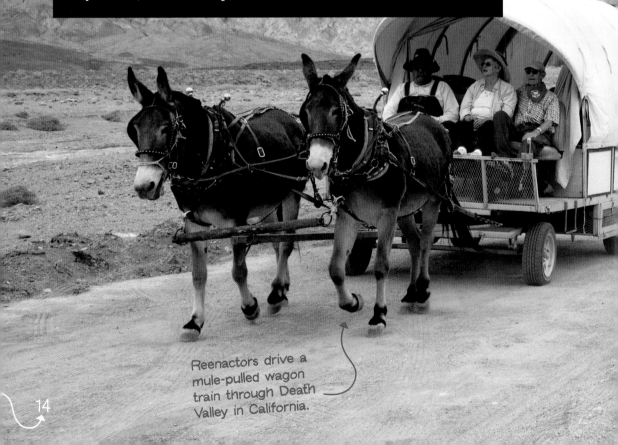

Reenactors drive a mule-pulled wagon train through Death Valley in California.

Horses are fast and strong, but they don't travel well over rugged terrain. They're also pretty fussy eaters and need lots of fresh water and regular rest. Oxen are strong, but they're not very fast. And they eat a lot. Mules, on the other hand, are hardy and can travel far and wide. Their strong legs and tough hooves can easily handle a rough trail or a crumbly hillside. They can carry heavy packs (bundles of supplies tied together for animals to haul). And they'll eat just about anything. On westbound trails, mules ate tree bark and dry grass. They were also known to chow down on rags, hats, decks of cards and, at least in one case, a wagon belonging to the U.S. government.

Still, mules have their drawbacks. They're known for, well, mulishness. They're mighty stubborn. And back in the West, they outsmarted many an inexperienced traveler. They escaped from corrals, ditched riders, and came up with endless ways of resisting pack loading. And if a mule decides he doesn't want to do something, good luck changing his mind. An old saying claims that mules *can* run as fast as horses— they just won't.

Did You Know?

A mule (left) is a hybrid. That means it's bred from two different animals. A mule is the offspring of a male donkey and a female horse. Mules don't occur in the wild. They have to be bred by humans.

Did Cowboys Really Wear Big Hats, Chaps, and Boots?

THEY DID. Cowboys wore big hats to keep the sun off their faces. They wore chaps—heavy leather or fabric pieces that fit over trousers—to protect their legs from thorny bushes. Their boots were well suited for horseback riding. They had tall heels that could hook on to stirrups.

Cowboys needed all this special gear because they spent most of their days—and often many nights—outdoors. And they did much of their work on horseback. Cowboys worked on ranches, many in Texas. Ranches are large farms for raising cattle. Cowboys moved from ranch to ranch, wherever there was work.

The 1870s were the heyday of the cowboy. Back then, most ranches were open range. That means the cattle roamed free over large areas. It was a cowboy's job to make sure the cattle always moved to places where they had plenty of grass to eat. Cowboys also watched to see that cattle didn't wander off, get hurt, or get stolen.

In the fall, cowboys rounded up the male cattle, called steers. They drove the animals along trails to towns such as Abilene, Kansas. The steers were loaded onto trains bound for big cities, where they'd end up as someone's steak dinner.

By the 1880s, Texas and other parts of the West were filling up with pioneers. Most Texas pioneers were farmers and sheepherders. They needed fences to protect their crops and flocks. The battle was on between fenced-in farmers and open-range cattle ranchers. In the end, ranchers lost. Most ranches became smaller operations with fewer cattle. Cowboys took permanent jobs as ranch hands. Some settled down on their own small pieces of land.

Did You Know?

Some books and movies cast a cowboy's horse as his best and trusted friend. But most open-range cowboys didn't own their own horses. Horses were supplied by the ranch. Cowboys did, however, own their saddles. A good saddle was a cowboy's most prized possession.

This early-twentieth-century cowboy poses with his most prized possession—his saddle.

Did Native American Chiefs Wear Feather Headdresses?

SOME DID. But the West was home to many different Native American groups, from the Tlingit of the Pacific Northwest to the Comanche in the Southwest. Each group had its own language and traditions—including what they wore.

Lots of old photos and movies show Native American chiefs wearing long or circular headdresses made of feathers. Those headdresses were worn by Plains Indians, such as the Lakota, the Cheyenne, the Crow, and the Blackfoot. But they weren't worn only by the leaders of these groups. All experienced warriors wore them.

A Cheyenne man wears a long feather headdress in this late-1800s photo.

The headdresses were made from eagle feathers. Native Americans admired eagles for their power and skill in hunting. Each time a Native American warrior showed himself to be strong and brave in battle, he was given a feather for his headdress. A chief could also earn feathers for leadership and for helping others.

In addition to feathers, headdresses could be decorated with beadwork, metal disks, and ribbons of colored cloth. Chiefs and warriors mostly wore their headdresses for ceremonies. They usually didn't wear them in battle.

Modern Native Americans still wear feathered headdresses at ceremonies and gatherings such as powwows. Some Native American groups award eagle feathers to male members who have served in the U.S. military. Or feathers are given to Native American men who have done good deeds for others.

A Sioux woman dons ceremonial clothing in an image taken around 1899

Men Only

Native American women sometimes fought alongside men in the Wild West. Modern Native American women also serve in the U.S. military. But women don't wear feather headdresses. Headdresses were and still are considered men's items. Women have their own ceremonial clothing.

Did Swarms of Grasshoppers Attack Pioneer Farms?

YES! Many times in the 1800s, huge clouds of grasshoppers appeared in the summer skies over the Great Plains. As horrified farm families watched, the buzzing, spitting insects landed on trees, crops, and gardens, eating everything in sight. They banged against cabin windows, got into water supplies, and stained bedding and clothes. The bugs hit people in the face and eyes and crawled up skirts and pant legs. Gross, huh?

The 1870s were a particularly bad time for grasshopper plagues. From the Dakotas to northern Texas, swarms of the insects destroyed crops. The grasshoppers also laid eggs in the farm soil, so new bugs could attack the following spring.

But grasshopper swarms were only one of the many natural disasters that pioneers endured. The Great Plains have extreme weather conditions.

Grasshoppers weren't the only danger for farmers. This tornado ripped through Oklahoma in about 1898.

Winter blizzards dumped many feet of snow, blocking roads and even railroad trains. Hailstorms and tornados struck in summer. Long periods of hot, dry weather caused prairie fires and dust storms. A hard, sudden rain could cause flooding.

Pioneers dealt with all these problems without modern equipment and without emergency services. The hardships were too much for some settlers. They packed up and moved back East. But most pioneers stayed, relying on themselves and on their neighbors to get through hard times.

Did Stagecoaches Really Get Robbed and Attacked on Their Way West?

THEY DID SOMETIMES.

Maybe you've seen this wild chase scene in old cowboy movies. A stagecoach pounds full-speed along a dusty trail. Behind it are some bandits or angry Native American warriors. They're in hot pursuit of the stagecoach, and they're gaining on it. The terrified passengers hang on for dear life while the trusty driver does his best to escape.

Scenes like this really happened in the West—though they weren't as common as old movies would have you believe. So what's the truth about stagecoach robberies? Let's take a closer look.

Before coast-to-coast railroads were built, most pioneers traveled by wagon. Some families traveled in their own covered wagons. But other westbound travelers took stagecoaches. Stagecoaches were run by companies. For a fee, passengers (and a limited amount of their luggage) rode west from one stage station to the next.

Stagecoaches also often carried U.S. mail and money.

This fact attracted the attention of bandits. To protect the valuable cargo, some stagecoach companies hired guards or used the U.S. military to watch over their stagecoaches.

Native Americans also attacked stagecoaches, but not to rob them. Beginning in the mid-1800s, Native Americans saw more and more settlers coming west. Some groups were angry that the settlers were moving into Native American hunting grounds and taking over their land. A few groups sent bands of warriors to attack stagecoaches (and wagon trains and, later, railroad trains). But these attacks weren't frequent. Stagecoach companies simply avoided trails that led through hostile Native American territories.

Bone Jarring

Stagecoaches were built to travel over tough trails. They had large wheels and a sturdy brake system. The light coach body sat on leather strips called thoroughbraces. The thoroughbraces were the suspension system. They kept the solid parts of the coach from slamming against one another. Still, stagecoaches bounced and

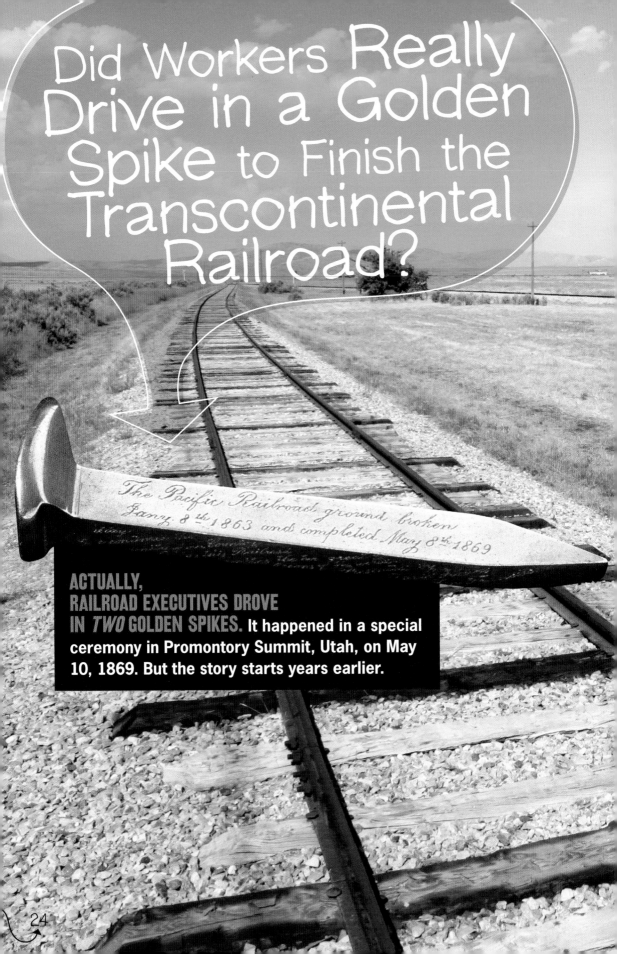

Did Workers Really Drive in a Golden Spike to Finish the Transcontinental Railroad?

The Pacific Railroad ground broken Jany. 8th 1863 and completed May 8th 1869

ACTUALLY, RAILROAD EXECUTIVES DROVE IN *TWO* GOLDEN SPIKES. It happened in a special ceremony in Promontory Summit, Utah, on May 10, 1869. But the story starts years earlier.

In the mid-1800s, railroads connected eastern cities. But no cross-country lines existed west of the Missouri River. About 1860, a young engineer, Theodore Judah, began plans for a transcontinental (crossing the continent) railroad. On such a railroad, settlers could travel from the east coast to the west coast in days instead of months. Some problems stood in Judah's way, such as the solid granite Sierra Nevada. But he was not discouraged.

Luckily, the U.S. government agreed with Judah's idea. In 1862 President Abraham Lincoln granted two companies the right to build railroads on U.S. land. On the eastern end, the Union Pacific (UP) began building in Nebraska. The Central Pacific (CP) began in California.

At first, work was slow due to the Civil War (1861–1865). But when the war ended, many young men took jobs with the UP. On the western end, the CP hired Chinese laborers by the thousands. It was a race to the center, with both companies aiming to lay the most track.

The race took on a life of its own. In 1868 the two railroads went right past each other, laying tracks almost side by side for 200 miles (322 kilometers). They would've gone on too—but the government finally said, "Enough!" Everybody backed up and agreed to meet in Promontory Summit.

At the May 1869 ceremony—originally scheduled for May 8 but postponed until May 10—CP and UP executives drove the golden spikes into the last rail. The CP locomotive *Jupiter* met the UP's *Engine 119*, symbolizing the link between the East and the West.

Finish

All Aboard!

In 1870 almost 150,000 people bought tickets on the transcontinental railroad. Rich people traveled first class. They paid one hundred dollars for a four-day journey. They sat on upholstered furniture and ate fancy meals. Poorer folks, many of them immigrants, traveled third class. That cost forty dollars and took ten days. Third-class riders sat on wooden seats and brought their own food.

Were Most Railroad Workers in the West Chinese?

YES! This fact may surprise you. When you think of the West, you probably think of white cowboys and Native Americans. Chinese immigrants might not come to mind. But Chinese immigrants played a very important role in the settlement of the West.

By the 1850s, more than fifty thousand Chinese immigrants had moved to California. Most were young men. They'd come looking for work in California's gold mines. When construction began on the transcontinental railroad, the Central Pacific hired a small group of Chinese men. Despite racism against Asians, the workers made a good impression. Soon 90 percent of the CP's construction workforce was Chinese.

To build their part of the transcontinental railroad, the CP had to deal with the Sierra Nevada. The CP couldn't build up the mountains' steep slopes. The railroad had to go through the mountains. But blasting roads and tunnels out of solid granite wouldn't be easy.

Over centuries, the Chinese had perfected the art of making fireworks. Railroad bosses thought they could put that knowledge of explosives to use in tunnel blasting. Crews of Chinese workers were lowered on ropes down the sides of mountain passes. They stuck explosives in cracks in the rock and lit the fuses. Then they yanked on the ropes. It was a signal for workers above to pull the baskets before the explosives went off. If crews at the top didn't pull fast enough, the explosives workers were killed or injured.

By May 1869, the transcontinental railroad was nearly complete. In a ceremony on May 10, eight Chinese workers were chosen to lay the CP's final 10 feet (3 meters) of track. The honor was given to a Chinese crew to symbolize the role they had played in linking the East and the West.

Clean Living

Many railroad workers were hard-living types. They drank a lot of whiskey, got into fights, and didn't take care of themselves. But the Chinese workers ate lots of vegetables and fish. They usually drank only tea. And they took regular baths and kept their clothes clean. Their healthful lifestyles meant they rarely needed time off for illness—which thrilled their railroad bosses.

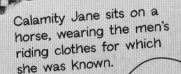

Calamity Jane sits on a horse, wearing the men's riding clothes for which she was known.

Was Calamity Jane a Real Person?

SHE CERTAINLY WAS. Calamity Jane is one of the most famous figures of the Wild West. In a time when women didn't have a lot of freedom, Jane went where she wanted and did as she pleased. She wore men's clothing, swore a lot, and handled horses and guns like nobody's business.

Calamity Jane was born Martha Jane Cannary in Missouri in the early 1850s. Not much is known about her early life. According to some stories, Jane's family moved to Montana in the 1860s. Both her parents died soon after. By the time Jane was in her early teens, she was on her own.

Jane got a job as a scout for the U.S. Army. A scout is someone who knows the natural landmarks and trails in a territory. Scouts were hired by wagon trains to guide settlers through the West. The military also hired scouts to gather information about Native Americans. Jane became well known for her courage and lively spirit.

The discovery of gold in the Black Hills of South Dakota brought Jane to the town of Deadwood in the 1870s. While there, Jane saved a stagecoach under attack. And when smallpox (a serious infectious disease) swept the town, Jane nursed many residents.

In the 1890s, Jane joined Buffalo Bill's Wild West Show. This troupe of gunslingers, scouts, and cowboys performed riding,

Deadwood, South Dakota, was a bustling gold rush town in 1876.

roping, and shooting tricks for big-city audiences. But Jane drank too much alcohol and got into too many fights. Buffalo Bill was an old friend, but he had to fire her.

Jane returned to Deadwood, where she died in 1903. By that time, she was already a legend, thanks to dime novels (cheaply printed books) filled with stories of the rootin' tootin' West.

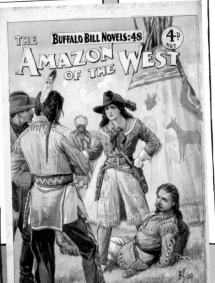

Calamity Jane (center) and Buffalo Bill (right) were often featured in dime novels.

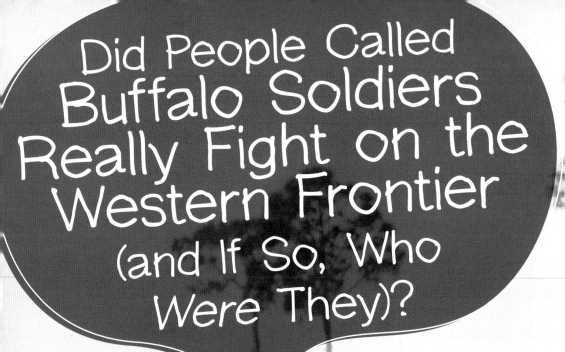

Did People Called Buffalo Soldiers Really Fight on the Western Frontier (and If So, Who Were They)?

Buffalo soldiers stand at attention in this photo from the 1890s.

YES, MEN KNOWN AS BUFFALO SOLDIERS DEFENDED WESTERN TOWNS FROM ATTACKERS. **They also guarded railroads and stagecoaches and fought against Native Americans. The buffalo soldiers were part of the U.S. Army. They were made up of four regiments (military units) of African American soldiers. These soldiers joined the army after the Civil War.**

Before the war, it was common for African Americans to be held as slaves in the South. But after the war, President Abraham Lincoln and the U.S. Congress made slavery illegal. The end of slavery improved conditions for African Americans. But they still often found themselves with no homes or jobs. And they faced racism and limited opportunities. For young black men, the army promised regular pay, regular meals, and someplace to sleep. The army even offered education and a chance to move up through the ranks.

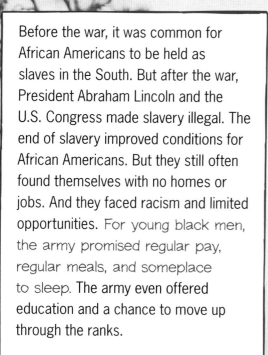

Henry O. Flipper was the first African American to command a buffalo soldier regiment.

Buffalo soldiers endured a lot of hardships. They wore the uniforms of the U.S. Army, but that didn't spare them from bigotry. Buffalo soldiers also worked long hours in the harshest frontier conditions. Yet the buffalo soldier regiments had the highest enlistment rates (number of people joining) in the frontier army. They also had the lowest number of deserters (soldiers who leave the army without official permission).

But how did they get their name? Historians think that Native Americans called the regiments wild buffalo. The Native Americans said the soldiers were tough and hard to bring down during battle, like buffalo. The name stuck.

Did Native Americans Use Every Part of the Buffalo They Hunted?

You may have heard that Native Americans took care not to waste the buffalo they killed. And it's true! **THEY REALLY DID USE ALMOST EVERY PART.**

Buffalo (also known as bison) were the main source of food for Plains Indians such as the Kiowa, the Lakota, and the Cheyenne. These groups also used buffalo hides to make tipis (tentlike shelters) and clothing. They made tools from buffalo bones.

Until the mid-1800s, tens of thousands of buffalo roamed the Great Plains. Enormous herds of the shaggy beasts grazed on prairie grasses and small shrubs. Large and tough, the buffalo had few natural enemies except for the occasional wolf pack.

Native Americans hunted the buffalo for centuries before Europeans came to North America. At first, Native Americans hunted on foot. Then Spanish settlers arrived in Mexico, bringing horses with them. Native Americans learned to ride horses and use them for hunting. Successful buffalo hunts supplied food and necessities for the whole year. The buffalo was so important that it became part of some Native American legends.

In the 1850s, white settlers began hunting buffalo in huge numbers. They took only the buffalo hides to ship back East for clothing. They left the meat to rot. By the 1880s, most of the Plains buffalo had been killed off by white hunters.

Without the buffalo, Plains Indians had to give up their traditional way of life. They were forced to take up farming.

In the 1890s, the U.S. government took steps to protect buffalo in Yellowstone National Park. The buffalo remain protected there and in several other areas from Oklahoma to Montana. Under this protection, buffalo herds have grown.

A woman in Montana scrapes an animal hide in front of her tipi.

Pemmican

Have you ever heard of pemmican? It was the original energy bar. Native Americans made pemmican from buffalo (or deer or elk) meat. They dried lean cuts of meat and then pounded them almost to a powder. The meat was mixed with animal fat and dried berries. The mixture was packed into rawhide bags. Pemmican lasted for months and made a nutritious meal on the trail or on the hunt.

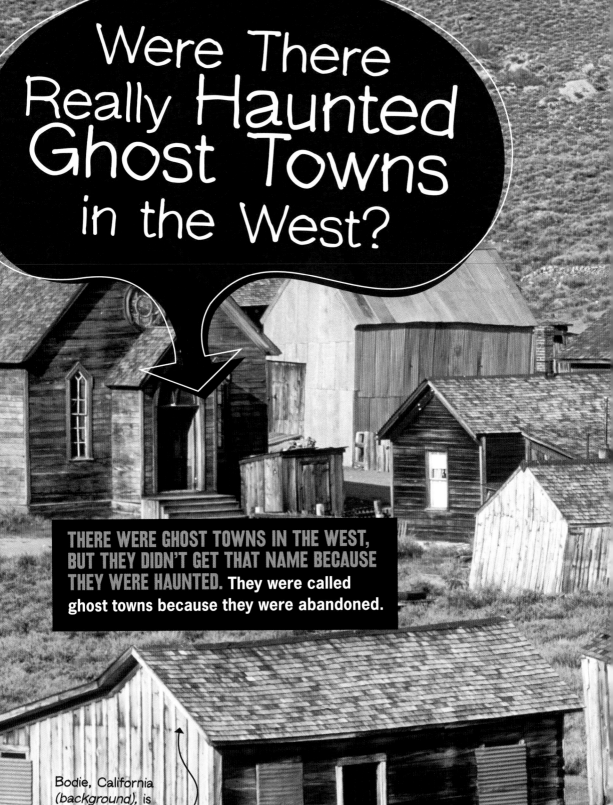

Were There Really Haunted Ghost Towns in the West?

THERE WERE GHOST TOWNS IN THE WEST, BUT THEY DIDN'T GET THAT NAME BECAUSE THEY WERE HAUNTED. They were called ghost towns because they were abandoned.

Bodie, California (background), is a ghost town in the West.

Many western ghost towns are the remains of boom towns. Boom towns were places where buildings went up quickly. People moved in by the hundreds to start new jobs and lives.

How did the towns go from boom to boo? Well, many boom towns sprang up almost overnight. If the railroad was putting down tracks in an area, a town would soon develop there. If gold was discovered on a patch of land, a town suddenly appeared. These towns provided food, lodging, supplies, and entertainment for workers and visitors.

Some boom towns, such as Tombstone, Arizona, grew especially fast. But sometimes the source of jobs and income dried up just as fast. If the railroad decided to bypass the town or the nearby mines were emptied of riches, people moved on. If enough people left, the towns just up and died. Stores stood empty with their signs clanging in the wind. Houses were abandoned with the curtains still hanging in the windows. Lonesome and left behind, these spots earned the name ghost towns.

Now, that's not to say the West had no actual ghosts. If you're of a mind to believe in such things, the West has plenty of tales of haunted places. Places with a haunted reputation include the Bird Cage Theatre in Tombstone; the Alamo in San Antonio, Texas; and the Maria Teresa Restaurant in Albuquerque, New Mexico.

GENERAL STORE

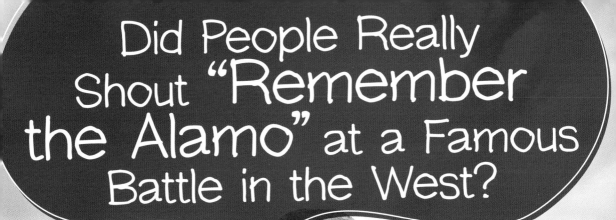

Did People Really Shout "Remember the Alamo" at a Famous Battle in the West?

THEY DID! You may have heard the phrase "Remember the Alamo." And you might know that it has to do with a battle in the West. But do you know who shouted the famous battle cry? Or why they shouted it? Or when?

The Alamo

It happened at the Battle of San Jacinto in Texas on April 21, 1836. On one side of the conflict was a group of Texans. The Texans were U.S. and Mexican settlers. On the other side was the mighty Mexican Army led by General Santa Anna. The Texans were fighting the army because Texas was a part of Mexico. The Texans didn't have the freedom to govern themselves. And the Texans wanted to be free.

It was the Texans who shouted "Remember the Alamo!" They shouted it as they charged the army at San Jacinto. They did so in honor of an event that took place just weeks earlier—the Battle of the Alamo. The Alamo was a group of buildings that had once been a mission, or religious center, in San Antonio, Texas. In their fight against Mexico, the Texans had used the Alamo as a fort to protect their volunteer soldiers and their families. From inside the fort, the Texans held off the

Texan soldiers defeated Santa Anna and the Mexican Army at the battle of San Jacinto in 1836.

Mexican Army for thirteen days. But on March 6, 1836, Mexican soldiers broke into the Alamo. They killed all but two of the Texan fighters inside.

Things went much better for the Texans at San Jacinto. They won their war against Mexico. Texas became an independent country in 1836. In 1845, it became a U.S. state.

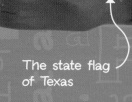

The state flag of Texas

GLOSSARY

bandit: an armed robber

buffalo soldier: an African American soldier who defended western towns from attackers. Buffalo soldiers were part of the U.S. Army.

chaps: heavy leather or fabric pieces that fit over trousers. Cowboys wore chaps to protect their legs from thorny bushes.

Civil War: a war that was fought between the North and the South from 1861 to 1865

corral: a fenced-in lot for keeping horses and other livestock

epitaph: a saying written on a gravestone

fort: a building used to protect soldiers and other people against an enemy

forty-niner: a name for a person who took part in the California gold rush of 1849

frontier: the farthest edge of a settled territory

ghost town: an abandoned town

Great Plains: a large area of central North America. In the United States, the Great Plains extend from the Mississippi River to the Rocky Mountains. Much of the Great Plains are prairie.

immigrant: someone who moves to another country to live

marshal: a police official

mission: a building or group of buildings used as a religious center. In the 1600s and 1700s, Spanish Christians ran many missions in parts of the West.

mule: the offspring of a male donkey and a female horse

pack: a bundle of supplies tied together for an animal to haul

pemmican: a traditional Native American food made of dried meat mixed with animal fat and dried berries

pioneer: a first or early settler in a new territory

prospector: a person who searches for precious metals

ranch: a large farm for raising cattle

scout: a person who knows the natural landmarks and trails in a territory. In the Wild West, scouts helped guide wagon trains. They also helped the military.

sod: dirt held together by grass roots

stagecoach: a horse-drawn passenger wagon that made regular stops

tipi: a tentlike shelter used by some western Native American groups

transcontinental: crossing a continent

SELECTED BIBLIOGRAPHY

Brash, Sarah, ed. *Settling the West.* Alexandria, VA: Time-Life Books, 1996.

Conlan, Roberta, ed. *The Wild West.* New York: Warner Books, 1993.

Kallen, Stuart A. *Life on the American Frontier.* San Diego: Lucent Books, 1999.

Sheinkin, Steve. *Which Way to the Wild West?* New York: Roaring Brook, 2009.

Smith, Robert Bar. *Tough Towns.* Guilford, CT: Twodot, 2007.

FURTHER READING

Brown, Susan Taylor. *Enrique Esparza and the Battle of the Alamo.* Minneapolis: Millbrook Press, 2011. Read about the experiences of Enrique Esparza, a real eight-year-old boy who survived the massacre at the Alamo. An eight-page reader's theater script accompanies the story so that you can act it out.

Hicks, Peter. *You Wouldn't Want to Live in a Wild West Town! Dust You'd Rather Not Settle.* New York: Franklin Watts, 2002. Find out what life was really like in the Wild West—and why you probably wouldn't have wanted to live there yourself!

Markel, Rita J. *Your Travel Guide to America's Old West.* Minneapolis: Twenty-First Century Books, 2004. Markel takes readers on a trip back in time to explore the Wild West.

Murdoch, David. *North American Indian.* New York: DK, 2005. Striking historic and modern photos highlight the histories of Native American groups.

Nelson, Vaunda Micheaux. *Bad News for Outlaws: The Remarkable Life of Bass Reeves, Deputy U.S. Marshal.* Minneapolis: Carolrhoda Books, 2009. Nelson tells the story of Bass Reeves, a deputy U.S. marshal in the late 1800s and an African American hero of the West.

Tombstone, Arizona
http://www.tombstonechamber.com
The official home page of Tombstone, Arizona, includes pictures of the town as well as a live Tombstone webcam.

Way Back: Gold Rush
http://pbskids.org/wayback/goldrush/index.html
Check out this site for information on the California gold rush, the forty-niners, and famous historical figures affected by the gold rush.

INDEX

ACKNOWLEDGMENTS
The images in this book are used with the permission of:
© Lonely Planet/SuperStock, p. 1; © Nancy Carter/North Wind Picture Archives, pp. 2 (top), 9; © Werner Forman/Topham/The Image Works, pp. 2 (bottom), 18; The Granger Collection, New York, pp. 3, 19 (top), 21, 24 (inset); The Art Archive/Bill Manns, pp. 4, 17; © Cameron Davidson/Stone/Getty Images, p. 5; © Bettmann/CORBIS, pp. 5 (inset), 13 (inset), 28–29, 29 (top); © Justin Guariglia/National Geographic/Getty Images, pp. 6–7; © Huntington Library/SuperStock, p. 8; © Nativestock.com/ Marilyn Angel Wynn/Collection Mix: Subjects/Getty Images, pp. 10–11; © iStockphoto.com/Xiangmin Zhang, p. 11; © George Eastman House/Archive Photos/Getty Images, pp. 12–13; © Jan Butchofsky/CORBIS, pp. 14–15; © Andy Crawford/Dorling Kindersley/Getty Images, p. 15; © Hiroyuki Matsumoto/Photographer's Choice/Getty Images, pp. 16–17; Library of Congress, pp. 19 (bottom, LC-USZ62-55811), 33 (LC-USZ62-46967); © Theo Allofs/The Image Bank/Getty Images, pp. 20–21; © Travel Library Limited/SuperStock, p. 22; © Buyenlarge/Archive Photos/Getty Images, p. 23; © iStockphoto.com/tness74, pp. 24–25; Courtesy of the California History Room, California State Library, Sacramento, California, pp. 26–27; © Alpswen/Dreamstime. com, p. 27; The Art Archive/Buffalo Bill Historical Center, Cody, Wyoming/19.74.64, p. 29 (bottom); © Underwood & Underwood/CORBIS, pp. 30–31; Photograph of Henry Flipper, 1877, HR 56A-F23.3, RG 233, Records of the U.S. House of Representatives, National Archives, p. 31; © Paul E Tessier/ Photodisc/Getty Images, p. 32; © VisionsofAmerica/JoeSohm/ Stockbyte/Getty Images, pp. 34–35; © Royalty-Free/CORBIS, 36; State Preservation Board, Austin, Texas, p. 37 (top); David Buffington/Photodisc/Getty Images, p. 37 (bottom).

Cover: © Comstock/Getty Images.

Lerner Publications Company
A division of Lerner Publishing Group, Inc.
241 First Avenue North
Minneapolis, MN 55401 U.S.A.

Website address: www.lernerbooks.com

Library of Congress Cataloging-in-Publication Data

Kerns, Ann, 1959–
    Was there really a gunfight at the O.K.Corral? and other questions about the wild west / by Ann Kerns ; illustrations by Colin W. Thompson.
        p.   cm. — (Is that a fact?)
    Includes bibliographical references and index.
    ISBN 978–0–7613–6100–8 (lib. bdg. : alk. paper)
    1. West (U.S.)—History—19th century—Miscellanea—Juvenile literature. I. Thompson, Colin W., ill. II. Title.
F591.K44 2011
978"02—dc22   2010011815

Manufactured in the United States of America
1 – CG – 12/31/10